for the love of the journey

for the love of the journey

Excerpts and insights for mindful, healthful living...with LOVE!

Kirsten Tonja

for the love of the journey
Excerpts and insights for mindful, healthful living...
with LOVE!

Copyright © 2015 by Kirsten Tonja

The author of this book does not intend for any of its content to be construed as medical advice. Please consult your physician or health coach before implementing changes with regard to your health/diet.

ISBN: 978-0-9962713-0-1

1st addition, April 2015

Self-Help/Motivational & Inspirational

Printed in the United States of America

This book of love is dedicated first and foremost to my husband and partner through this life, Quincey. Your infinite support and acceptance of all my wild and crazy ideas and reaching of unreachable dreams is ever-inspiring. I love you...infiniti!

To my mother, Lois, the loving Being that supports unconditionally with few questions: you always know in your heart that anything I set my sights on attaining is absolutely within my reach, mostly due to your help in an abundance of ways...all of which I am thankful for daily. I also feel inclined to thank you for reading to me from birth and encouraging me to read throughout my childhood. That is, without a doubt, the best thing anyone has ever done for my intellectual and emotional evolution. I love you!

To my father, Dennis: thank you for making things right and for proving every day that you are the kind of big-hearted and generous man that you were born to be. Though you may mask your giving heart behind a rough exterior, I know, undoubtedly, that it is your most beautiful attribute. I love you!

To the Ookies: I started loving one and got two...then I got 2 more in the form of twin godsons! You are my chosen family for a lifetime. We always have each other's backs, in good times and in bad. Your strength and support are assets in my life. I love you all so much!

To my brother, Jason: though your are no longer an Earthly part of my life, your light and smile shine on me daily and for this I am eternally grateful.

To Emily: I had just begun my awakened journey and

then I met you. My life has never been the same. I attribute so much of the person that I am today to you and the love and guidance you've shown me on a daily basis since our first meeting in 2006. I love you!

To my Kindred Spirit, Renee': time and distance may keep us apart but we are forever in each other's hearts. Like Buttah!

To Wader: I miss you and know that you would be giving me some sort of Ayn Rand/ethical egoism lecture right here, right now, but I would let you go on all day if it meant I had just 24 more hours with you. I love you!

To Fred: It's not about the destination; it's about the journey...even if it meant having to listen to Journey way too much! Though our destinations are far off from one another, our combined journey put me here...in the Present Tense.

To each and every friend and family member that has put up with me, my craziness, my indignant rants: every moment spent with each of you has written my story...a story that I love and cherish because of the characters in it. From dance floors, desert raves, band gigs and island parties to high school, workplace meetings, cafe encounters and road trips, you all fill my heart with peace, love and happiness.

To every author of every book that I have read or will ever read: THANK YOU!

Bless up!

Contents

~ Chapter 1 ~
Love

Love is King!

Let's forget the masculine nature of the word 'King' for all intents and purposes which I am about to mention. In the accounting world, one of the primary philosophies (or principles, if you want to get technical) revolves around cash. Cash is King. And while there may actually be some heated discussion in the financial world as to whether or not that is truly accurate, there are many cases in which that statement is used with precision. Of course, in business one might expect that the almighty dollar rule the rhetorical roost. I'd like to take a look at the word 'King,' taking it out of the specific "ruler" perspective and checking in with another defined scenario: Chess!

The definition of 'King' within the confines of the game of chess, according to Oxford Dictionaries, is as follows: *"the most important chess piece, of which each player has one, which the opponent has to checkmate in order to win. The king can move in any direction, including diagonally, to any adjacent square that is not attacked by an opponent's piece or pawn."* Now let's use the word 'Love' in place of 'King' and assume that the game of chess really refers to life. How cool is that? Love is King! It is why we are here. It is the whole point. Love of Self. Love of Others. Love of the Earth. It all makes sense, doesn't it? Let's spread our Love King around this huge chessboard called life. Before we know it we will find our collective check-mate and it will be beautiful!

The process of checkmate will entail taking out the cheaters/frauds (Rooks), the clergy (Bishops), the armed forces of all kinds (Knights) and those blindly following in ignorance (Pawns)...all with Love, obviously. Likely so, 'taking out' really means conquering. In spite of thoughts to the contrary, Love does conquer all.

Don't think that I forgot about the Queen! Oh the darling most powerful piece in the game. King is most important, you see, but no King reaches full potential without a Queen. We have designated descriptions for all of the other pieces on the board. Let's define the Queen as passion, for really, isn't love synonymous with compassion? Compassion means to suffer together...with each other.

It would suffice to say that passion is an integral part of compassion. Passion moves fluidly around the board in any straight direction as far as it can until meeting its own. Likely, the Queen is doing a fair share of spreading passion; a powerful emotion used in tandem with love, which can ultimately rule the Universe.

So here I sit proposing that cash is not King in the least. Who cares about cash? Is it not just pieces of worthless paper? A virtual dollar amount in the cloud of the Internet? Nothing of reality. Why would cash be King when Love clearly carries all of the value in life?

"All living things flourish when they are loved well. If you want to cultivate growth and healing, love without an ulterior motive and success is subsequently imminent."
~Kirsten Tonja

The only way to have a prosperous and plentiful garden is to love it well. You may feel that tending to a garden, planting seeds and seedlings, watering them and weeding around them, isn't the kind of love we show our spouse, children or other family members but really? Is it not the same? And the fact that it *is* the same makes it that much more sensible that we would strive to live our lives through our heart center and show love to every living Being that we come in contact with on a daily basis. We are able to exhibit love to that which we create, that which we nurture, that with which we are connected. Are we not connected to each other? Are we not connected with Nature? Are we not connected with the Universe? *Yes,* we are! Why not approach every waking moment from a place of love? We are capable of showing the same love to a perfect stranger as we are to our spouse or our pet...why not live each day in love?

We allow so many minor annoyances to distract us from our higher purpose and rob us of our Presence. So much wasted time is spent hating on that guy that cut us off on the highway or that person that worked their way in front of us at the deli counter. So, they set us back some time but why also give them the power to set us back in Presence?

The key to success in your life, your career, your passions, is to love. It will work itself out after that. Don't believe me? Hey, far be it for me to tell someone to exclusively believe something they heard, saw or read. Go ahead, do your own scientific experiments. It is possible, you know? Conducting your own experiments about how certain things, activities, foods or even television shows make you feel is a real demonstration of taking the power into your own hands.

When you are beginning to fume about a situation, notice it, Be Present, change your course and be kind. Say something nice, smile, whatever it takes. Then observe how that makes you feel. Observe for the rest of the day. On the flipside, if you jump off the handle, observe how that makes you feel. Truly pay attention to your thoughts, feelings, your physical demeanor and even how your body feels. It will change your outlook. You will find that if you abide by those profound immortal words spoken by Patrick Swayze's character "Dalton" in the movie *Roadhouse*, you will be on your way to a better day...better days. "Be nice until it's time to not be nice." One may debate when it would be time to not be nice but honestly, being nice is the best recourse 99% of the time.

Once you live a love-filled life and come from that heart center first and foremost, the shift you feel will be amazing, beautiful and even sometimes chilling. Everything gets clearer about the choices that you are supposed to make and the road that you are supposed to take. That's success, gushing from your Spirit, calming the fears, suffocating the self-deprecating thoughts and quelling the mental chatter! Seize every day. Make living a love-driven life your reality. Take all of your passions and confidently form your actuality, your success. Every smile goes a mile and every frown brings you down. It's only a matter of time before your wins increase and you are able to carve out another ring of love, just like those gorgeous rings within a tree...which come from a life affected by love.

The Earth's love makes nourishment and growth possible. It doesn't always require optimal conditions either. All it takes is a mutual understanding of what it requires to help one another thrive. We can go around surviving or we can focus on thriving. Too many people dwell on simply surviving. How many times do you hear people say things like "You'll survive" or "I'm a survivor?" Why obsess on sliding by in survival mode when we can love and thrive? Thrive in love! Humans have a tendency to make situations much worse than they actually are. It's time that we learn how to harness love in every moment to the greater purpose of our success!

JourneyTweets

"Every smile goes a mile and every frown brings you down."

@kirstentonja #ftlotj #journeytweets

Spend time with animals and feel the love. Or...how I learned about unconditional love from my doggies Jane and Lucy!

I have spent much time lately observing Lucy. Lucy is the doggie child of my husband and me. She is a Boxer and I would argue that the entire breed is a lesson in love in itself. Lucy is our third Boxer. Our first passed away mid-2005. We had just gotten our second, Jane, because we thought Roxy was lonely. It turned out that she had cancer that took over her whole body. She was five-and-a-half years old when she died. We quickly learned that Jane was deaf and she proved to be a challenging puppy but grew into an incredibly sweet and cherished companion. When Roxy died, we got Lucy, as Jane was more of my husband's girl and I was distraught about losing Roxy. Enough time of grieving had passed and I became ready for a new addition. The two dogs traveled across the country with Quincey and I four times. They saw more of the United States than many humans and acquired many friends along the way. We have friends all over the country and many of them spent quality time with our girls and us. They were the highlight of house parties and a comfort in low times. Not a day has passed since having a dog in my life that I haven't thought about the infinite love they have to give. Have a bad day? Go home. Get *love*. Immediately.

Jane recently passed away at the beginning of

November 2014. It was a traumatic exit with a stroke and then seizures directly followed by what we believe to be a heart attack. She died in my husband's arms. She had just turned ten on Halloween. She thrived with cancer for five years. She was a blessing every day. She had many quirks even outside of the breed that made her incredibly special and endearing. When she died, we all took it hard. We don't have children. The doggies have always been our kids. Lucy clearly missed her "Sister." Lucy got sick and we soon discovered that she had Lyme disease. After a heavy dose of antibiotics, she bounced back. Shortly thereafter she took a tumble down some steps and got stuck. Again, she bounced right back. Quincey and I both realized that she too was displaying her age. Lucy will be ten in May 2015. If you know the breed, ten years of life is pretty impressive, so I regularly focus on how blessed we are to have had Jane in our lives for so long and to still have Lucy. We didn't feel right leaving Lucy at home alone anymore. She only knew life with Jane. We started taking her everywhere and only left her home if we were going to be away two hours or less. In this I have learned even more about the ever-present loyalty she has shown us.

Dogs have awesome senses. I cry. Lucy comforts. I am sick. Lucy comforts. I need a friend. Lucy is always there. She is the one living Being that can do no wrong in my eyes. She has an accident. Hey, it's only carpet or flooring or...who cares. She does nothing that makes me mad or even irritates me and that is because though she does not speak she says everything and that everything is all love. I would even go so far as to say that in the past five months she has supported my emotional well-being so much that I couldn't possibly begin to show enough thanks for her always present love and all around gentle goodness.

It's not just dogs though. Different strokes for different folks. I could probably spend a day with a cow or an elephant or a giraffe and discover those same loving traits. To me, cats are sneaky, but my parents have some of the sweetest cats I have ever known...all cats that someone didn't want at various times and decided to drop off in the rural area where they live. The compassionate people that my parents are, they always end up taking them in...the unwanted misfit toys given a second chance to shine, and shine they do.

You may not have the space or means to have a pet but try to make some time to spend with animals. Discover that love of a different kind. It will always make your day better.

~ Chapter 2 ~
Success

Luck has nothing to do with joy or success. *We* create our own reality. Live by design rather than by default. There is so much energy swirling around us, and let's be honest, a lot of it is not pleasant. The important point to remember is that negative attracts negative and positive attracts positive. We each are literally creating our own reality. If we are focused on how much we hate our job or say things like "if it's not one thing; it's another" or "if it weren't for bad luck, I'd have no luck" that's exactly what we are creating for ourselves.

Take some time to think about how often you say things like this in your life and how much it continues as you say these types of statements more and more. Before you know it, you have an enormous snowball of negativity taking you down more like a wrecking ball.

On fear. Or...what is holding me back and how can I release that pattern?

The patterns of living Beings are a great source of amazement. The patterns in Nature. The pattern in our psyche. The patterns of someone with OCD. The daily pattern of routine. What can we learn from a pattern? Patterns are a fine representation of the past. Just look at the rings on a tree or the Fibonacci spiral on a head of Romanesco or that same spiral on the outside *and* inside of a pinecone. There is a breathtaking background to the patterns in nature...an aura of purity, of a life of oneness. What about our patterns? Human patterns. These are the intricacies that keep us in the past. For example, addictions: they keep people in the mire of wallowing in the past until that pattern is so ingrained that it's a hard habit to break. What was that quote on insanity again?

"Insanity: doing the same thing over and over again and expecting different results."
~Albert Einstein

Yeah that one! The pattern, embossed on our brain that keeps us in the same self-destructive circles. Perhaps the infamous 'rescinding the drive before it gets too fast' is the culprit this time? That self-sabotaging moment when you quit before you give yourself the chance to actually succeed? Fear: always use it as a roadmap for the direction in which you absolutely *should* go.

JourneyTweets

"Fear: always use it as a roadmap for the direction in which you absolutely should go."

@kirstentonja #ftlotj #journeytweets

"Ever tried. Ever failed. No matter. Try Again. Fail again. Fail better."
~Samuel Beckett

Oh those words, the duality. Failure. Success. What if the real fear is of success rather than failure? Life changing, right? It really is. People tend to think of failure with fear. Often, we struggle with failure and even the thought of failure so much that it eats away at us to the point that we don't know how to even deal with it anymore. But, what if the struggle is actually with that poignant thought of success? It almost brings chills to my spine.

Is it the extra work, feeling like your success will bring you overwhelm and give you less free time or that it will cause a host of other problems such as money, fame or a general lack of privacy? Those are the kind of feelings that we don't often register as the reasons why we are afraid to pursue our passions. The spotlight is so heavy on the "failure" part that we neglect to realize that we are merely afraid to shine!

Think about what you would be doing with your life and your career; how would you be living your making if you didn't have to worry about money? How does this make you feel? Imagine that feeling in the pit of your stomach and with your whole heart. How would you take that feeling and make it real? What would you do to get the wheels in motion? Well, do that then! Are you "stuck" in a job you hate? Do you feel trapped and unable to escape because of debt, responsibilities and who knows what else? There is no time like the Present! We are all capable of making changes...even while we are in our "cookie cutter day jobs." If you are delaying, if you are making excuses, it just may be because you cannot accept your own bright shining light, your infinite greatness. Get over it! You are beautiful. You are amazing. You are Love. You are capable of all of the successes that your Heart and Soul desire. Don't let the fears take over!

Here's the thing: you must start focusing on you and what makes you happy. Our feel good emotions must be alive and thriving in order to bring more of that tingly feel-goodness back to us. Feel it! Don't fake it till you feel it. *Really* feel it. It's not difficult to think of something that makes you feel insanely happy. Hold that within your Spirit and just marinate in it. Wrap your heart, mind and Soul in that sentiment. It feels awesome. It can be as simple as how it makes you feel to pinch your doggie child's squishy cheeks, get a kiss from your lover or hear your child say the words "I love you!" It can be that feeling that a cookie made by your mother can give you while you are eating it. Hold it! Yes! Hold that feeling. It's real. It's true. It's the beginning of carving a new way of life for you!

This is a lot to digest but the simplified version is that if we are to live happy lives, abundant lives, we are required to learn what life is truly about. It all starts with Love. Think about Love whenever you have to cope with uncomfortable situations or feelings. We are capable of changing our journey in life. In an instant, we can tap into our energy Source and take the reigns. Why let life just pass us by? Why allow fear (which includes guilt, anger, jealousy, greed, hatred, etc...) control our path to righteousness. I'm not talking about biblical righteousness; I'm talking about the righteous righteousness, dude. It is our birthright to live a life that we love and to love the life that we live. It all starts inside and radiates outward. It becomes first nature...just as it is divinely meant to be.

I look around and see so many people focusing on that negative...that negative vibe. It's only bringing you down, baby. You can continue the madness of emitting negative energy but the only result is attracting boundless negatives. Our energies swirl around us. It's not solely our energies though. It's the energy of everyone, everywhere: the positive and negative energy of all living things. You put out your negative energy and it is bound to expand with more from others. You know what that means? Now you don't just have your negative crap...you are attracting everyone else's as well. Ain't that grand? I don't know about you but I would much rather be putting out the loving good vibes into our collective air space. You pickin' up what I'm puttin' down?

The real talk is that if you are insistent on reiterating all of the negative in your life and being knee-deep in the land of complaints, you are just going to have so much more to deal with...all in the form of an abundance of terrible occurrences followed directly by the unhealthy obsession of all that sucks in your life.

"You can only become truly accomplished at something you love. Don't make money your goal. Instead, pursue the things you love doing, and do them so well that people can't take their eyes off you."
~Maya Angelou

"What do you do for a living?" My usual answer is "the minimum amount necessary to get by." I mean... the truth is, that answer really embarrasses some people. I once met one of my brother's coworkers and the first and only question he asked me was what I did for a living. I could see the embarrassment wash over my brother's face after hearing my response. I guess it sounds awful to a lot of people. Many assume that kind of attitude means laziness. Not so. I just really don't see that what someone does "for a living," meaning their job or career, is a jumping off point to a quality conversation. Where I worked at the time surely did not define who I was or tell much at all about me. I like to enjoy life. That doesn't mean that I am not a hard worker. I just choose to do the minimal amount of conventional-type work. I like the nonconformist minimalist lifestyle.

In 2007, I was in my second year of working for a tech startup company in San Diego. I worked full time for one company and did part-time work for another company owned by the same person. That year I made just under $100,000. What happened to all of that money? Rent was $2,000 per month; I had a $400 monthly car payment; gas was super expensive and so was (is) food. Utilities are all more expensive in California. I did buy some material things (but not really that much), high-quality dog food for two sixty-pound dogs, gardening supplies, soil and seeds, music and music-related expenses, books. The problem was that I was working tons of hours both in the office and at home and I wasn't even getting to enjoy any of that big money. Working for oneself is so much more rewarding and enjoying life and nature is how I make a living. But really, I'm just living my making.

~ Chapter 3 ~
# Presence

On Being Present. Or...gaining access to and fluent use of your unconscious.

Our unconscious actually runs the show. We have to tell it what to do or think. If we think or do negative things, it runs with that. If we shine positivity, our unconscious goes that route. Our unconscious is the great creator of growth. Growth comes through challenges...physical and metaphysical. So, it pushes us to evolve. We can do amazing things if we just learn love and release all judgment. Staying Present really facilitates this. Let yourself be guided!

JourneyTweets

"Stream of consciousness: In which direction are you rowing?"

@kirstentonja #ftlotj #journeytweets

Breathing/Meditation

The optimal way to Be Present as much as possible is through conscious breathing and meditation. There are many different ways to meditate and it really comes down to what resonates the most with you, specifically. The key is to take the time to work through what works best for you and to stay faithful to a daily practice. A ten-to-twenty-minute meditation session daily coupled with pointed breathing techniques twice a day will produce results quickly. Dr. Andrew Weil offers multiple refreshing, anxiety-quelling and sleep-assisting breathing techniques on his website. Check it out; you won't be sorry!

Gratitude journal exercise

This exercise will remind you, even on the worst of days, of all for which you have to be thankful! Each night, write all of the good things that happened to you during that day, all of the nice things people said to you and did for you. It is an awesome activity to show how blessed you are and how incredibly fortunate you are to be living the life you love and loving the life you live. Try it! It only takes a couple minutes. Do it before bed and go to sleep with a smile on your face!

"Our intuition knows from birth. It's our condition that takes us down the confusing corridors of life's labyrinth and jumbles up our purpose, disguising it as something to be bought or at the very least, die coveting."
~Kirsten Tonja

For the love of the journey. Or...what's your why?

Ever notice how children insistently ask "why?" Why do they do that? And...why do parents and non-parents alike seem to get so annoyed with the exchange of "why" questions?

Kids ask "why?" because they instinctively know. They know "why?" is how to get to the core meaning of the matter. Of life. Of everything. Of Spirit! It's not about the "what," the "how," the "when" or the "where." The nitty-gritty answers always come from "why?"

We have spent our entire lifetime being intensively conditioned to be what others desire us to be (which would explain our Spirit-crushing annoyance with the pertinent question of "why?"), act how others want us to act and to consume the way others want us to consume. What a joke! Let's be honest here. It's a ploy to keep pockets of the rich lined with more and more gold. To really take back our lives, all we need to do is get back to our Self, our Love and our Self-Love. Think about something that ignites a spark of passion. You can find your heart within that spark by asking "why?" Why are you so passionate about doing this thing or going to this place? You can run down through the other questions, too, if it helps you to also figure out the "why?" This is what children do. Something catches their attention and immediately they go to the "why?" Then the Spirit crushing starts. Tossing the questions aside as some trite nuisance, only giving them a moment of attention and rarely giving them an honest-to-goodness thoughtful response are all ways we handle the inquisitive child. It only grows from there. This phenomenon occurs our whole lives as we stray so far away from our "why" and focus straight on the obsessive traits that lead us astray and keep us from fulfilling our true potential. Our true potential has nothing to do with money or power, prestige or charisma; it is about being authentic and loving, feeling abundance and providing illumination. All of these things being brought to you by the letter "Y?"

Our intuition knows from birth. It's our condition that takes us down the confusing corridors of life's labyrinth and jumbles up our purpose, disguising it as something to be bought or at the very least, die coveting. The innocent minds of babes have it right on mark. Then...life happens. That's the kicker though. The life that the majority of us human Beings know is not at all the real Life. We're getting there though. We are finding our fire and spreading the sparks. We are throwing the flames of "why?" out into the Universe and it is creating something ever-so-beautiful. Love is becoming abundant and more easily accepted. We shall not shun the development of our Spirit. Our reason for living is to find our "why?" and to know that it will only come from a place of Love. Through forgiveness and compassion towards ourselves as well as others, we will hold the space for growth and introspection...always finding out "why?" We have to give 100%. This isn't to be dealt with like it's some kind of minutiae. It requires work. We must do the work.

The serious difference between this work and the

kind of work we don't necessarily feel great about is that this work is infinitely rewarding and always cathartic. The way to happiness always starts within. Why? Because examining our thoughts, emotions, feelings and actions and their alignment with each other (or lack thereof) is how we figure out what feels pleasant and what does not. When we feel pleasant and fulfilled, we pass that feeling on. We pay that Love forward. We do not obsess over that which we shouldn't control. We release the willingness to focus on the negative occurrences in our lives and the insistence that luck and hope have anything to do with...well, anything.

Start today! The next time a child asks you "why?" no matter how many times in a row, answer those "whys" with piquancy. Really, the next time *anyone* asks you "why?" refrain from feeling it burdensome but rather embrace it as a pertinent lesson in which you are supposed to participate. You may find you are surprised at the end result and inspired to begin your quest of "why?" Once it goes down like that, you can never go back to the way it was. The enlightenment has been activated. The "why?" will come.

JourneyTweets

"Think about something that ignites a spark of passion. You can find your heart within that spark by asking why?"

@kirstentonja #ftlotj #journeytweets

~ Chapter 4 ~
Community
&
the Universe

The Universe always has my back. Or...releasing my need for control.

It is so difficult to liberate ourselves from our own restricting behaviors. I have found the recurring behavior that gives the most angst to be that nasty desire to always have control. If anyone had told me that ten years ago, I would have scoffed at them. I would have gone on some tangent about how society needs more control and that if parents controlled their children more, we wouldn't be in this predicament. I would have spouted off about controlling weight, controlling taxes, controlling anything you can actually control. Five years ago, I would have talked about controlling corporations, politicians, any officials in public office, controlling food policy, GMO's, environmental destruction and most certainly controlling how we react to the fact that we are being controlled. Yet here I sit in 2015 and the one trait I find to be most burdensome for myself is my need and will to control. I used to work to control schedules, meals, routines...to go forth in a manner that allows for everything to have its place and to *definitely* be in that place. How adorable of me to think that life has been drilled down to something so simply stated as "control yourself and your life."

Graduate from high school, get a job or go to college and then get a job, marry, buy a home, settle down, have children and live that American dream. Work that forty-hour work week, put your kids in daycare and subsequently public or private school. Control it all. Merely reading back the words I just wrote makes me cringe. While it may be acceptable for many, I abhor that this is what has been instilled. I fought the concept. I fought "the man." I still fight to vote with my dollar, but the reality is that as long as we are focusing on all that is not right with the World and our lives; we are in a constant wrestling match with control. We can be passionate about the plights that ignite that spark and we can walk the walk to go along with the talk. The real deal, though, is coming to peace with our Being and living every moment in the Present tense. We can form dreams and strive to reach goals but if all of that is done through blinders, what have we to live for? When we resolve to feel fulfilled and consistently acknowledge abundance, we start to really understand the value in our life. It's this material World we are living in that has torn our Spirit to tiny pieces. No matter, designer clothes and shoes, game consoles, television and Hollywood gossip will keep us occupied. Crime shows preying on our fears and commercials marketing anything and all the things will further reinforce that need to control every detail of our lives. Be safer. Be cuter. Be smarter. Be better. Then you can be happier.

Screw that. Turn off the television and release that mindset...then you are headed toward true freedom. Do things. Be with nature. Take your shoes off and walk in the grass. Stop scheduling everything and remember that everything does not always have to be put away in its place. We compartmentalize as much as we can when we should be addressing, feeling, doing...continuing with Presence. Live each moment in a real state of Being and you will find that your triumphs, worries, dreams and downfalls will all be in the hands of the Universe and will find their way to the proper compartments all on their own. This is not to say that we should-n't try and strive, that we shouldn't have drive and mo-mentum, that we shouldn't pay any mind to the future. It simply means that we should pay more mind to the now and know that all things will happen as they are supposed to happen in accordance with our greater pur-pose. We must remember our Earthly purpose is to help one another, to love each other and to Be.

The great design of the Universe always empowers and inspires if we simply allow it to do so. The way in which we are able to do so is by Being here now. We must show up and be open. It *absolutely* requires us to release the incessant compulsion to have all things as we think they should be and all people doing what we think they should do. It's all about you. Not them. Not that. Not it. You. Right now.

"Once you make a decision, the universe conspires to make it happen."
~Ralph Waldo Emerson

Synchronicity is such a dazzling phenomenon. I love this Emerson quote because I find that, for me, it directly relates to synchronicity. The meaningful coincidences that happen to us, which could be easily overlooked if we are treading in the past or barreling toward the future, are a force to be reckoned with. Synchronicity can be something as simple as thinking about or singing your favorite song, which comes on the radio soon thereafter. It could be thinking about a friend and then getting a call, text or email from them in the same day. It could be a dream that reveals as some form of reality within coming days and it could be that symbol or sign that you use to move forward in one way or another showing itself, perhaps blatantly but often in a more obscure fashion. In Health Coaching, synchronicity often occurs when you, yourself, struggle with a certain habit or addiction and then someone calls you for a consultation that is struggling with the very same issue. Frequently, we make decisions on how we want to live our lives, what we do or don't want to do, eat or drink but we still struggle with the ingrained addictions. Along comes someone with the same tussle and suddenly you realize that the Universe is helping you towards your desires by throwing you an opportunity to coach as well as learn. It's divine.

It's crucial to not take the substantial synchronicities for granted. Being Present helps us to be on point when these moments occur...to say "a-ha, there it is" and to embrace what is intended for us to ascertain. The Universe, ever-conspiring to make our intentions turn to reality, is our best friend. Why then do we sabotage the outcome? That's the tendency, at least, with human nature. It's that negative energy rearing its ugly head again. It can easily go the other way, however. All we need to do is notice, acknowledge and continue to scrupulously proceed with confidence in the direction of our goals and aspirations. It can be tricky with so much anger, fear and melancholy swirling about but it is *so* worth it.

I'm sure many of my peers will beg to differ, saying that their dreams rarely come true despite their best, most valiant efforts. I strongly urge a reexamination of the "have-not" attitude and suggest working towards affirmations and truly setting intentions. Be nice. Show compassion. Don't simply seek out money, fame or power. Those are empty reasons for any outcome. There has to be more. We are capable of doing well while doing good and if we set out to do just that, the Universe unites for our cause. It doesn't mean you can't strive for financial stability. It simply means that it shouldn't be the only focus. It's so much easier to live the life you love and love the life you live when you keep this concept in tow.

A great way to put your intention to action is to be clear about it, to write it down, to workshop it and really pinpoint how you want to make positive change in this World while at the same time pursuing your passions and being monetarily independent. It's not only beneficial in general, but it is also therapeutic.

We have a choice. We can wander aimlessly through our lifetime or we can rock it. We are all here for a reason; we just need to discover our purpose. It's within us. We just have to peel away those layers, much like an onion, and find it. It's time to pull it together and accept our destiny. The "what-ifs" are the worst. No one feels too hot when thinking about something they didn't do because they were afraid. Peeling that onion is a courageous act and it can be scary, traumatizing for a time and especially daunting. That outcome though. Yowsa. That amazing feeling when you have had the veil lifted, you have discovered what life is *not* about and therefore are learning what life *is* about. It can involve tears, screams, feeling of helplessness and hopelessness, but the consistent self-exploration and self-improvement make a huge difference in a short amount of time and provide multiple servings of gratification and gratitude. It also assists with feeling mentally, physically and spiritually more aligned with Nature, the Universe, the collective community and our Self. Let the Universe be your guide!

Note: For more information on the concepts of synchronicity, peeling away layers of our consciousness like an onion and collectivism, check out the written works of Carl Jung.

~ Chapter 5 ~
# Food
# &
# Mindfulness

A book discussing my ideas for mindful living surely cannot ignore the topic of food. Food is the one thing that we have absolute control over in our lives. While I would typically argue for releasing the need for control as much as possible, this is one topic for which I stand firmly on the "heck yes" side. Control those food choices!

We hear a lot these days about healthy food being too expensive. It's one of the biggest arguments in favor of the fast food mania that exists. However, I beg to differ. I counter with the blatant fact that many people do not want to take the time to prepare their own food anymore.

I did some research for this topic and the average two person food total at any given drive-thru is about $20 (or more)...for one *terribly unhealthy* meal! I avoid fast food because I strive to nourish my body with healthy foods and I focus on eating a rainbow of plants. My husband and I own and operate a vegan plant-based cafe and we certainly provide that same price point...all healthy...all organic. More so, it can just as easily be accomplished with a short amount of time and less money in one's own kitchen.

I used to proclaim being a Vegetarian. I even adamantly worked towards Veganism...and then I just stopped labeling. I also found myself experimenting with foods, plants and animals alike. Without a doubt, I thrive on plants, but I have also come to appreciate a piece of wild-caught sockeye salmon from time to time...or chicken, turkey, eggs or raw cheese. Don't get me wrong, it is quite infrequent but I consciously decided not to label myself any longer. It took me awhile to learn this and to lean into it, but I know that everyone responds to individual foods differently. The bottom line, though, is that the meat industry is responsible for some serious water usage.

I am an avid conservationist when it comes to the H2O, and the outrageous amount of water it takes to produce one pound (yes, one pound) of beef makes me want to cry. How many gallons of water does it take, you say? Two thousand five hundred gallons is the number. When I think about the amount of pounds of beef that the typical American eats and break it down into those water usage numbers, I want to fall to the floor flailing my arms in a tantrum. This is no longer about taste or nourishment; this is about the literal selfishness involved with excessive livestock consumption...especially in a time when we don't need to be so gluttonous as there is plenty of other food available. Not to mention: our bodies cannot digest such large amounts of meat properly (you know, those giant slabs of steak or one full pound burgers)...nor can they handle meat every day, every meal.

Listen, I know everyone is in a big fat hurry these days. We take that trip around the Sun faster each year, it seems. But, if we are not mindful of how we nourish our Earthly machines, how are we to be mindful of anything else? And if we are not mindful about how our consumption influences our one and only Earth, we are missing a humongous point of it all.

I know this sounds a little preachy. Trust me when I say it is much less preachy than I used to be. I focused on activism of all sorts for many years and I also spewed forth a lot of indignant rants. Those rants did have quite a bit of shock value, but they didn't go nearly as far as the gentle, loving nudges that I now pursue. This just happens to be one of those non-negotiable items. We are running out of water. The production of meat for food (and not just factory "farming" but also "sustainable" farming) is the number one water hog. Pun intended. It uses exponentially more water than the filthy fracking industry...which says a lot. We need to get a grip on this before it is too late. It doesn't take radical changes to make a major impact. It's time to focus more attention on Mother Earth and less on our ever-expanding waistline. Let's do our part right now to Be the change!

This chapter will take a trip along a high level path of easy ways to nourish that body and enjoy the process. Some of these ideas and exercises are so easy that you will find yourself wondering why you haven't been doing them all along.

Mindful eating with a moment of gratitude. Or...how to eat for pleasure and purpose.

"Your body is precious. It is your vehicle for awakening. Treat it with care."
~Buddha

I recently saw a social media post with a linked article about a restaurant or cafe that offered a discount to those that took a moment to be thankful for their meal. Of course, the masses came forth crying foul and pushing the agenda that this is discrimination towards people that do not hold religious beliefs or participate in prayer. The sad part about this is that you don't need to believe in God, a god, deities or any Higher Power to take a minute or even just a couple seconds to give thanks for being able to eat. There are so many Beings in this World that don't have the basic necessity of food; why not pay respect to our impending meal?

Sometimes I forget but for the most part, I begin each meal with a moment of gratitude for what I am about to eat. I think about the nutrients that my body is receiving and how tasty everything is going to be. Being an avid plant-based foodie, a nutrient geek and someone who is extremely comfortable in the kitchen, I also focus my attention on certain ingredients and what, exactly, they are doing for my body and how they aid my overall bodily functions. I should play devil's advocate with myself here and say that I also acknowledge when something I am eating isn't that great for my body but delicious nonetheless. I always remember that if we treat our body right most of the time, it can easily deal with and bounce back from a sinful treat from time to time. It's no fun to be such a staunch supporter of one certain and rigid diet or lifestyle! We are all so different and our body chemistry is unique to us. One precise diet does not work for every single human Being. And if we are always limiting ourselves, the temptation is all the greater. The thing about "diets," not to be confused with the word "diet" which merely refers to what we eat, is that they limit so much that it sets said dieter up for failure. It is our nature to want what we can't have, to long for things we know aren't best for us...but we can change this perspective if we spend time with our food. By "spend time," I mean carefully selecting ingredients and washing, cutting and preparing them, whether raw, steamed, juiced, blended, sautéed, dehydrated, baked or otherwise. This is where the true connection takes place. The current system is completely removing this crucial piece, with other people preparing our food (or food-like substances in many cases), the rapid pace of the drive-thru and the "I need it now" mentality; we are totally missing the point.

So, I have outlined a bit of what I see as a problem but I have also offered up solutions. We don't need to spend hours on our meals for them to taste delicious. We also don't need to go out and spend more money on terrible food choices (for the sake of time and convenience) than we would if we just did it ourselves. It's hard to start if you have no idea where to even begin. But hey, oh the Internet! What a beautiful thing! And hello! Pinterest and YouTube can help you with anything! Simply allow your curiosity and creativity to flow by typing an ingredient or two into the search field and delight in amazement at what your query yields!

Another pertinent part of mindful eating refers to our consciousness and our surroundings. Do you eat while sitting in front of the television or at your desk at work? Do you take the time to enjoy your meal or do you wolf it down like you are in a contest against the clock? Here's the thing: we need to chew our food much more than we actually do in this fast-paced society. Chewing activates digestion. When we take a bite and chew it a couple times before swallowing, we don't send adequate triggers to the many parts of the whole system involved with digestion. Chewing also relaxes our stomach muscles. This makes food move with more ease through the digestive tract. Obviously, chewing turns our bites of food into smaller pieces, which also helps make the entire process easier on our body. Both the mechanical and chemical processes that take part during digestion commence with chewing! There are serious implications that stem from improper digestion, everything from reflux to bacterial overgrowth and more.

More than the logistics of digestion, chewing helps us maintain the Present moment while we are eating. It pushes us to remain in that state of Now and appreciate every morsel. If we take the time and relish in all of the goodness that comes from a nutritious, well-balanced meal, we can harness that energy all the way through to our next meal. It's all a matter of maintaining mindful appreciation of the journey of the meal rather than the destination of a clean plate.

Another method to mindful eating is using chopsticks! I know it sounds crazy and people sure do look at me funny when I pull a pair of portable chopsticks out of my purse and use them when dining out, but it works. No matter how you look at the situation, using chopsticks during your meals rather than a fork, means you are going to spend more time chewing between bites while you set up your next bite with those tricky chopsticks! Even better if you aren't that great at using them! It makes for a challenge, but it gets to be "normal," is always fun, aids in digestion and creates an atmosphere that stays true to the Present.

JourneyTweets

"It's all a matter of maintaining mindful appreciation of the journey of the meal rather than the destination of a clean plate."

@kirstentonja #ftlotj #journeytweets

Plant-based

Plant-based is where it's at! I'm not going to sit here and type a sermon on why we shouldn't eat so much meat (though more on the topic will come up later). It suffices to say that we all truly know deep in our hearts that the majority of our food (A.K.A. source of nutrition) should come from plants. Yes, those lovely living leafy creatures that grow in dirt are the key to sustained health, infinite energy and mega nutrients! Again, I am not trying to turn the World's inhabitants to Veganism or even Vegetarianism. The fact isn't that we should cut out meat; it's that we should go crazy eating plants... crowd out the meat! Eating a rainbow of colors of vegetables and fruits is the best way to maintain a healthy diet. Getting some beans and whole grains in the mix is great too. Hey, they come from plants too, you know! The idea is to consume mainly vegetables, some fruits, high quality fats and proteins...and of course, lots of refreshing water! A plant-based diet (again, that doesn't mean omitting meat completely, it just means focusing on plants) is also environmentally friendly and helps with water conservation. Leaving a healthy planet should be our goal as one whole community. Treading lightly and conserving for future generations surely seems like the appropriate action to take...especially if you have children! A little research on our part, some minor changes and a different set of lenses to look through and we can create our dream of a refreshing and healthy future for generations to come and all living kind.

Meat industry/Factory farming

I won't spend a lot of time on this topic. I decided that I would just skim through the main points and call it a day. You can read many of the books that I have by authors such as: John Robbins (heir to the Baskin-Robbins throne), Michael Pollan, Howard Lyman (you know, the guy that got himself *and* Oprah sued by the beef peeps), T. Collin Campbell, even Alicia Silverstone. You can grab books from vegan super athletes like Brendan Brazier, Scott Jurek or Rich Roll...all of which are enlightening and inspiring. I have been reading books about the veg/vegan lifestyle for roughly ten years. I am an avid reader. I love to study and am always down to learn new things. It took a lot of reading for me to actually embrace it. I still struggle with it, having been the perfect example of that Standard American Diet that everyone speaks about. I ignored a lot. I started my evolution on an intellectual level, followed directly by steadfast environmental activism and then it all spiraled. I got super involved and passionate about fighting the factory "farming" industry and reforming food policy. So here it is...

Time progresses and our votes mean less and less. With special interests, lobbyists and corporations that have it all and want to keep it that way, we don't have a lot of say. It's a stark reality. *But*...we do have a say in how we spend our hard earned dollars. Concentrated Animal Feeding Operations (CAFO's) and slaughterhouses are not only insidiously inhumane but also an environmental disaster. There's no longer any debate about how these animals are treated. We all know.

There's also not any secret about the antibiotic use and hormones which transfer to the humans that eat these meats. There's no doubt that this isn't any kind of quality life for all animals involved. Why then support it? Flip the switch. Change the game. Say "no" and create some real change. Fast food joints, chain restaurants, grocery stores and even most "mom and pop" food establishments are using factory-farmed meat. We have to take a stand. Compassion is of the utmost importance. Compassion for animals and respect too. Compassion for ourselves and our health. Those angsty energies from an animal's entire confined, miserable life and fearful moments of painful death are getting eaten by humans.

I don't know about you, but that doesn't make me feel good. Aside from the other health implications regarding the handling, cleanliness and packaging of dead animal flesh, there's the energy transference and the consumption of those nasty steroids, hormones and antibiotics. That's just with meat. I won't go into the gore of dairy but just simply ask this: how would you like to be taken away from your mother at birth? Or, how would you like to have your baby taken away from you at birth? It is a messed up situation. Look into better ways. It will exponentially change how you feel in your body and in your mind. Decrease consumption of animal meat and animal products too. We don't need it all...all the time. If there is any question, take it to YouTube. Perhaps you actually had no idea this type of abuse was occurring. Can you watch those undercover animal abuse videos and still stand by your food choices? It's worth some thought and introspection.

There is no doubt that in order to live a mindful life with love, we should not exclusively consider our Self, our family, even our fellow human Beings. It's integral that we consider every living Being. It is possible to make a difference and once we do, our lives, in turn, begin to change for the better. This is what being mindful is all about. This is what healthy living feels like. It's that understanding that though we live in what we once thought was a futuristic age, we don't have to immerse ourselves in it. We can still trust our Spirit and let Love be our guide.

Think (meditate) for a couple minutes with your eyes closed. Contemplate how you would like to live your life, what legacy you want to have left. Think about how you feel about animals. Do you have any pets? Do you consider your dog(s) and cat(s) to be part of your family? Do you get angry when you read or see news of abused pets? It's time to do some accountability housekeeping. How are those animals that you love any different than other animals? We can begin to take small steps and then branch out more and more each day, each week, each month. Before you know it, our dollar voting creates a whole new way of life...one that involves compassion for all living creatures.

Processed food and the corporations that get paid to make us sick

Think about this: How logical is it to eat from a box, bag or can? Consider your ancestral roots. Consider it biblically or from an evolutionary perspective...consider it both ways if you like. No matter how we look at it, the way modern society eats is a disaster...doing a disservice to our own bodies, our heritage and our Earth. The implications of the Industrial Age span much further than the size of our bellies or our ever-increasing sugar levels. The effects vary widely from air and water pollution to soil erosion to vacantly sculpting nature's perfect beauty into a soulless concrete jungle. We can heal this too! Again with that almighty dollar vote.

I can't possibly argue about the taste of processed food or all the foods that are so awful for our bodies. Much of it is delicious! It's not real food though, and it's not anything that our human body knows how to process. Digestion is an extremely refined and comprehensive process. It's meant to happen with ease...with real, nourishing food. Take whatever random artificial ingredient you want to pull from a box of almost anything from a major corporation in the grocery store and tell me that you honestly think our bodies will sustain digestion of these types of ingredients every day for a significantly lengthy lifetime.

It doesn't work that way...which is why Cancer, Diabetes, Heart Disease, Stroke, High Blood Pressure, Heart Attacks (the list goes on ad infinitum) are occurring at a much more rapid rate. It's not food; it's poison...and corporations are making tons of money while making us sick and making our Earth sick too. Consciousness involves making changes. Taking small, manageable, sustainable steps toward real food means a whole host of wonderful ripple effects.

I have spent enough time "fighting the good fight" with activism. I have spent nearly a decade speaking out. I have physically participated in protests. The real difference is made from within. The meaningful change starts with us, our food choices, our love of our Self and then branches outward. Think of some action steps you can take...three simple goals to work toward over the next week. Then build on that with three more the following week. It can be done and it can be fun! Save money. Be healthy. Be Love.

Sugar...the United States is on drugs.

I'm not sure if I should start this with the staggering statistics on Diabetes and the symptoms related to the dis-ease or the fact that sugar is eight times more addictive than cocaine. Well, I guess that solves that conundrum; throwing them both out right from the gate seems apropos. I won't bring out the sources. It's all very easily researchable. The data is readily attainable. And the denial is unfathomable. The worst of all culprits are drinks...every single kind of sugar-laden beverage. It doesn't make much of a difference if we are talking a can of soda, a bottle or box of juice, a coffee or energy drink or milk (yes, plain white milk). The average American is drinking an insane amount of sugar when what our bodies really need is water. Water: pure, refreshing, important. How is it that so many people don't ever drink water?

Also factor in all of the "foods" with sugar including the salty ones that people take for granted. Yikes. We are in a state of emergency. Sugar *and* artificial sweeteners have some truly gnarly effects on our brain and those effects carry through to the rest of our systems. It's a subject that needs some serious discussion, requires much education and truly begs for political reform. Let's be honest with ourselves. I'm not trying to cast a dark shadow on the positive energy of this book, but that reform isn't going to happen. There is way too much at stake for those with the money and the power. What can happen and will happen if we push hard enough is the change that occurs because we are no longer buying what they are pushing. Yeah!

Here it is again! Take the power of your dollar and use it for health and happiness. Cleanse the body and the mind of sugar and create a higher quality of life for yourself and those whom you love. It is totally doable. It may seem daunting and unrealistic, but all you have to do is make a list of small action steps. Do some research. Check out the statistics. Learn about those effects and gradually kick sugar to the proverbial curb. Before you know it, you will find yourself amidst a craving, caving in *but* quickly realizing that it's *way* too sweet. I use dates and maple syrup mostly, sometimes honey but no matter what, keeping all forms of sugar in check is the best scenario. I like to eat a little bit of fruit during a sugar craving. Root veggies like carrots and beets are also great to get through a crazed "I need sugar" moment. There are many other sweet vegetables to choose from depending on the season, and don't forget about some of the naturally sweeter tasting nuts and seeds! Over time (and not that much time, honestly) it starts to come with ease, become a healthy habit and is oh so yum!

Gardening!

Gardening is this amazing activity that you can do almost anywhere! You can have an herb garden in your kitchen, an urban garden on your back patio, a bigger suburban spread or a full acre (or more) of rural bliss. It's all equally satisfying! Once you get the itch, even if you start small, it grows into something that you don't even remotely want to control! Grow all the things!

The purest thing about growing your own food is that you start from a seed, nurture it, transplant it, weed, water, weed, water and boom...fruits of your labor of love! Results that you can eat...and healthy ones at that! It is such a natural pastime. Of course, we all have the innate desire to grow our own food, to be self-sufficient, to share the "fruits" with our community... our tribe!

I have personally found organic gardening to be a full-out game changer in my life. When I started the obsession, it taught me about tending to something that needed me. It taught me about a give-and-take relationship. I gave it my love, some water and overall TLC and it gave me food which I happily took...healthy food! I rejoiced in the results and did even more. The end result of food is a great motivator! I know what soil the plants were grown in. I know how they were nourished, what kind of water was used. I know that there were no toxins involved. It all begins as goodness from my Soul and ends with goodness in my belly. It does not get much better than that!

Growing your own food is a strong way to connect oneself with Nature, to live sustainably and responsibly and to create a compassionate community relationship. It would be so impressive if all members from each community got together and committed to sharing crops so that each person or family could grow just three or four vegetables or fruits that they excel at nurturing. To be able to hone your green thumb craft by growing the plants you enjoy growing the most while knowing that the community harvest will be abundant with variety, is like a slice of Eden.

Why not try it? Can you get together with some neighbors and build this concept? Even if we all were to grow veggies and trade harvests with one neighbor, that's the type of start toward changing the World!

~ Chapter 6 ~
Minimal Living/Clutter of Stuff

It is interesting when you start a spiritual and intellectual evolution. You begin to realize that all of your non-essential material possessions are controlling you. There are different levels of possession accrual...from minimalist to hoarder and everything in between. Collectors keep their collections in albums or curio cabinets or shelves. The collectibles rarely get touched, if ever. Maybe they get a bit of attention when a new piece is added. For less fancy collections that take up shelving, frequent dusting is required. What a pain! Then you have that moment when you say you like one certain type of animal or collectible and everyone and their baby daddy's sister's mother gets you those things as gifts for every occasion every year...until you have a full-blown community of Hello Kitty figurines or elephants or tea towels and you rue the day you ever expressed how beautiful that so-and-so was. It's fascinating to watch this phenomenon roll out. I have seen it in myself too, in the past, but once I resolved to keep it simple, my life changed drastically.

Stuff...it's pointless. It creates a burden. How many times have you had to move material items around when you are about to get company? How often do you grumble about dusting all of the crap on that certain shelf? It's no joke. Dusting is an endless and thankless task. You finally get to a breaking point and do it and the very next day...that ambitious dust is back! The biggest benefit of ditching the addiction to stuff is that you don't have to clean (or clean around) the stuff anymore! Hallelujah!

Perhaps the benefit that is even bigger than the relief

of physical clutter is the release of the mental clutter. When we have an addiction to stuff, to buying stuff, to keeping up with the clique, the neighbors, the trends, it really takes a toll on our well-being. Clearly, this is not what living to our fullest potential is all about. We cannot take it with us. Things do not matter. *You* matter. What you have done matters. How you have helped and inspired others matters. What you gave or got for Christmas that one year does not matter. All of my fondest memories in life are things that I have done. When I look back on my childhood, I feel so warm when I think about all of the projects that I worked on with my mom or the snow tunnels that I built with my brother, spending time in the woods all Summer with my neighbors and even playing Vanna White in home videos that my dad took of me showing his recently or soon-to-be restored old cars. I don't have prevalent memories of things. In fact, I can flip back through each major segment of my life and pinpoint memories of activities that I was doing with friends or family and that is what emotes love and joy and lifts me up.

It's time that society puts the emphasis of things in its proper compartment. Perhaps we should take the sentiment of collecting something and just put that in a curio cabinet? Why not write on a piece of paper how having another figurine to add to our collection is really going to change our core essence? While we are at it, maybe we can even stretch our brain to give some sort of existential meaning to our shelves full of dusty knick-knacks. Wouldn't that be much more enjoyable than dusting said knick-knacks daily, weekly or most likely monthly with a lot of grumbling, complaining and procrastination in between? I challenge everyone to take an honest look to determine which items you own really own you. This can also be applied to clothing, shoes, jewelry...you name it. It's a good possibility that you will start to realize how much you are being suffocated.

I should warn that once you start, it becomes very empowering. You begin to really appreciate the extra space to move and breathe. You realize how much money you were wasting on a lifestyle that in no way styles life. Take some time. Look around your home. Be honest with yourself. Do these things make you happy? Do they at all contribute to who you are as a Being? Is this the Self that you are overjoyed at having created? Do these items have anything at all to do with your values or consciousness? What you discover will likely change your life forever!

JourneyTweets

"You realize how much money you were wasting on a lifestyle that in no way styles life."

@kirstentonja #ftlotj #journeytweets

DIY Everything!

This is a topic that I am quite passionate about. I grew up in a family that made and fixed a lot of stuff. My dad restored and worked on cars and my brothers followed suit. Now it's my nephews that are into repairing anything that doesn't run. My creative talents don't necessarily flow mechanically but my better half never becomes defeated. It's amazing what we are capable of learning ourselves, if we really put our minds to it and use our resources. My husband and I have made everything we wanted to happen...well...happen. There is nothing that human Beings aren't capable of doing when we simply set our mind right with the task. Sometimes that does mean asking for help. Our pride gets in the way all too often, but reaching out to friends and family for help in pursuing your ambitions is courageous.

A great example of DIY awesomeness is the 2005 Toyota Prius that we drive. We got it at a junkyard. It was there because the hybrid battery was dying and the former owner, for whatever reason, decided to scrap it. We bought the car and continued to drive it for a full year before that hybrid battery completely died. Most people take modern vehicles to the dealer because of the highly computerized components, and we did spend $50 to have it hooked up to a diagnostic computer at the dealership in an effort to get a concrete answer of what was wrong. There is no way to diagnose certain codes independently which seems a bit off since you have to pay just to find out what is wrong with your vehicle, but hey, they get us coming and going...if we let them anyway. When we got our results, they insisted that the proper steps according to the diagnostics were to replace the hybrid battery and the cooling fan for the battery. The total cost for such a repair: $3,500. Of course, they quickly flipped the script to the fact that rather than spend the money on the repair, it would be better served as a down payment on a new car. I politely told them that that wasn't going to happen.

It's odd (and disheartening) when you really pay attention to how much of a disposable society we have turned into. No need to fix anything. Just trade it in or throw it away. Not us. We took the car and purchased a used hybrid battery online and replaced it ourselves. Well, I didn't do it but the amazing men in my life did. Quincey researched everything and boom. Just like that, the car was fixed for $900. Shortly after that a check engine light came on which can be diagnosed with a hand held diagnostic computer (usually for free at auto parts stores). Once we had the codes, the hubs took to the Internet and figured out what was wrong. We purchased a new cooling valve online, the men did the work...check engine light *off*. That fix at a dealer was $600. We paid $75. She runs like a champ now! I use this as an example because I know the usual response is "I can't do something like that" or "I don't know anything about *fill in the blank* to be able to make/fix it." My husband is not a car guy. He hates getting black grime on his hands. We are more the dig-in-the-dirt types. And my Dad isn't nearly as well-versed with cars with computers of any kind much less a Prius. The sheer will to learn, figure it out and push to a successful completion is all you ever need to do, fix or build anything.

You just have to believe you can do it.

We have learned/done everything from converting a decommissioned full-sized school bus into a beautiful mobile home to starting our own organic, plant-based cafe to farming the land using organic and sustainable growing practices. Even the creation, layout and publishing of this book is a DIY project. I can't begin to express the amazing feeling I get when I accomplish whatever wild and "impossible" feat I conjure. The most recent being the launch of my Health Coaching business...something that I am truly passionate about and quite adept at. I designed my own website, wrote the content, started writing copy for opt-ins, blogs, newsletters, workshops and more and ultimately, I keep pushing to learn every single day. I love working with people. I especially enjoy guiding people and creating space for the DIY aspect of changing their life for the better. We all have that power to make it happen.

It's crucial to remember that modern marketing from corporations hits heavy on us, pushing us to the brink of our apparent helplessness. It works, too. They really do a number on the consumer. The real talk is that we don't always need to pay someone to fix something or pay to replace something that no longer functions properly. Most items can be fixed and, a majority of the time, can be fixed without shelling out the bucks. Goals and ambitions can be figured out. Hobbies, crafts, talents of all kinds can be learned. We are capable of great accomplishments.

Think about some ways that you can put the DIY

mindset into motion. There's a good possibility that you already are! If you do your own fingernail grooming, cut your own hair or make your own laundry detergent, you are already on the path. Do you make your own clothing on occasion? Do you have a garden or chickens free-ranging in your backyard? Yes! That's the Spirit! It *is* possible to do it all, keep that mind sharp *and* have fun!

Reuse/Repurpose/Conserve

I'm going to dig right into this one. Humanity is exhausting the World's resources. We all know it yet very little is done about the situation. The amount of waste we collectively create is appalling. Recycling is one of those tricky subjects and certainly it is worth doing over perfectly recyclable items ending up in a landfill. However, it's to a point where we need to cease the disposable mentality. There is absolutely no reason to go to a coffee shop every single day and get your drink in a disposable cup if you know you are going to stop each morning. Why not take your own? Most places embrace that as it helps save money on to-go supplies...especially if they are a small business. Why is it that so many food establishments use one-use items? Think of all of the plastic bottles and containers and the Styrofoam (yuck!) that have no or limited recycle life. Aluminum and glass at least can be recycled over and over. And speaking of plastic, what is it even good for? Absolutely nothing but pollution, environmental destruction and an overall perpetuation of wasteful habits and poisonous toxins leaching into whatever the plastic vessel is housing. Things can only change drastically if we *are* the change.

We can alter our own habits and make an impact. We can share what we do with friends, family...everyone! Sometimes all it takes is gentle nudges and some insightful information for a person to realize that they don't want to be part of the problem anymore. How do we create the change? How can we Be the change? For starters, we can all learn how to reuse as opposed to tossing in the trash or recycling bins. We can take cups and containers to places where we get food and drinks instead of using one-use-ware. We can keep containers in our car for when we go out to eat and have leftovers. We can consciously think about what we consume and how that makes an impact. The amount of packaging involved with everything we buy compounded by the plastic bags that stores use to help consumers transport new purchases is incredibly wasteful. The plastic bags often end up taking a journey of their own right into our creeks, rivers, streams and ultimately oceans. I'll leave the research on this topic up to you, but do a simple web search on the North Pacific Gyre garbage patch and you will see why this is an environmental injustice. Our trash is ruining ecosystems around the globe and some-how the developed nations seem to not care one bit.

I know there are increasingly growing numbers of people who do care. I know that the consciousness evo-lution is happening. It suffices to say though, that the wasteful mentality is still strong and we need to push the envelope of change with fervor.

Repurposing has a great place in this conversation too. Giving something new life that otherwise would end up in the trash or at the curb on trash day is an en-vironmentally friendly, resourceful and fun way to live. It sharpens the creative juices and gives us an artistic outlet. Even faithfully shopping for secondhand cloth-ing rather than buying new keeps our creativity and originality fresh! Also a huge plus: not looking like everyone else is unbelievably empowering! Repurpos-ing in its name alone gives a sense of social and envi-ronmental responsibility. Turning that beat up old dresser into a "new" aesthetically pleasing and functional piece feels so satisfying!

Finally, I'd like to talk about water. We are running out of it, you know? California is in a dire situation and that's certainly not the only place in the World that has pressing water concerns. Corporations are bottling water, marketing it as fresh spring water and making a killing when the concept of bottled water is simply absurd in the first place. We flush perfectly good water down the toilet with our pee and poo. I can't tell you how many people I see on a regular basis waste water by letting the faucet run while washing dishes, brushing teeth, etc. And how about those long showers? This breaks my heart. Can you examine your water usage and make changes? I would be willing to bet almost anything that you can do better. We all can. Turning water off in the shower while soaping up and shaving, not flushing the toilet every time you pee and certainly not leaving water run...ever. It's so simple and yet it seems to be something that society is oblivious to and feels no social or ethical obligation to conserve.

I would urge that we all look within ourselves to find ways to do our part. One of those ways is to decrease meat consumption. There is no such thing as "sustainable" farming when it comes to raising animals for the dinner plate. I have already written about the subject so I won't repeat; I just wanted to put that reminder out there. Without a doubt, the most outrageous water usage occurs with raising animals for food...especially cows, pigs and other large livestock animals.

There is much for us to ponder in this life and to accomplish. It is our destiny to live from our Higher Self, do what is right for all living Beings and help one another...from a place of love. Let's do this! Together!

~ Chapter 7 ~

Wanderlust

wan·der·lust
noun
a strong desire to travel.
"a man consumed by wanderlust"

Whether you are a vagabond by nature or you have become more detached from material possessions and the physical World over time, wanderlust is a life-changing affliction *read: obsession* to have. Things never stay the same. And really, would a true vagabond have it any other way?

There is something to be said about the fact that such a large percentage of people never venture far away from the place where they grew up. More than that, many people travel to exotic islands, go on cruises or hit the main foreign tourist cities while ignoring (maybe even taking for granted) travel in their very own country. There is much to see in the States but we surely won't limit wanderlust to the borders of our own country. I'm not saying that being content with where you have always been located is a bad thing. Each person's comfort level is different and we are all our own unique individual Self. I will, however, examine one point that I find applicable to comfort and maybe even complacency.

"Great people do things before they're ready. They do things before they know they can do it. Doing what you're afraid of, getting out of your

comfort zone, taking risks like that- that's what life is. You might be really good. You might find out something about yourself that's really special and if you're not good, who cares? You tried something. Now you know something about yourself."
~Amy Poehler

It's so true, this quote! All of my greatest accomplishments are the ones that I was extremely scared to do but pushed forward regardless. That fear is what drives our personal/spiritual evolution. I guess I should actually say: the presence of fear perpetuates a resulting driving force. There are two choices and two choices only. You can feel the fear and run or you can feel the fear and proceed anyway. It's a recurring topic for me that links with all aspects of our lives, loves, activities, thoughts and growth. Just know that if you are feeling hesitation (often a result of fear), you will absolutely become a stronger person for going for that gusto rather than fleeing in fear and forever looking back on the "what-ifs."

This is where a wanderlust "affliction" *read: obsession* is a vibrant, beautiful thing. At first it is scary...going to new places, perhaps not even knowing the language. It could be a cross-country road trip or hiking the Pacific Crest Trail from start to finish, the fear is always going to bring forth an incredible rush. It's so easy to feel that rush of fear and get so scared that we retreat, but think of the times when you did feel the fear-rush yet kept moving. We all have moments like that...likely things that we were more confident about doing, but still fear-filled. Think about how awesome it felt when you did it though! The post fear-conquering elation is invigorating. Since most people do have at least one of those times readily retrievable in memory, we can hold on to that and use the recollection to persevere when we would rather crawl into a hole.

I look at the word "wanderlust" not solely with a literal definition of the word. Consider for a moment that friend or family member that regularly tires of doing the same job for too long or living in the same dwelling year after year. Maybe it's the college student that has changed majors seven times within their first two years of college. How about the entrepreneur that could never be content with just one business? And yeah, that couple you know that just has trouble staying in one area of the country too long before they are ready for a new adventure. I bet you know someone like that! Wanderlust, intrigue, creativity and drive all go hand-in-hand in creating a rich life filled with moments that build our character. Always be learning and pushing or become listless and stagnant. The latter certainly doesn't sound very enticing and though very few would admit to becoming such a reality, it is prevalent and rampant. Take a few minutes today and write down all of the things you can think of from your past that you didn't do because of the fear or resistance you felt. Examine how the exercise and reading through your list makes you feel. Are there any activities on the list that you wish you had done? Now list the times when you felt fear but did it anyway. How does this exercise make you feel? Lastly, write a list of things you want to do but currently fear. The final part of the exercise begs the question: What are you going to do with the rest of this life of yours?

Note: I emphasize the terms "affliction" and "obsession" when discussing wanderlust because there are those that consider wanderlust to be a full-blown affliction...something to be ashamed of, something undesirable. There are also plenty that consider it to be an uber cool obsession...lifestyle, state of mind.

Awaken to discover your true potential. Or…what it means to circumvent the confines of the matrix.

This World is full of stimulation for every one of our senses. Corporations, politicians and power players all know how to use this against us. We are constantly being targeted to be consumers of not just worthless possessions but also drugs (prescription drugs as well as street drugs), booze, television, trashy music, Hollywood, gossip, fashion, endless technology (which decreases our privacy but we still seem to be okay with that as a whole) and propaganda toward the persistent butting of heads perpetuating angst over that which we cannot agree. And we sure do not agree. Because of that, we find our passions turning into indignant soapbox speeches being typed spitefully behind a computer screen, and this ultimately does not work. It doesn't help anything or anyone and it essentially keeps us deeply rooted in that matrix. You don't have to wear a tin hat to know that the true purpose of life is being missed, ignored and twisted.

What do we do about it? We show up, work hard, are passionate and stay true to our art, to our creativity, to what pushes us to our Higher Self. Doing that nine-to-five thing and hating every minute of it is a disservice to oneself. Doing it because that's what is expected is preposterous. Taking our hard earned money from doing it and spending it on the mind-numbing Spirit-smashing aforementioned addictions is robbing us of our purpose and blinding us from seeing that truth within ourselves that so wants to shine.

It's no fun to stay drugged up. No matter if it's heroine or prescription pills, sugar or coffee, food or television, shopping or drama...they are interchangeable and they are wasting your opportunity to live the life you love and love the life you live.

What else do we put into motion to live with purpose? Write that book. Start your dream business. Go on the road trip you keep talking about. Ditch your possessions. Take a baseball bat to your television. Clean up your addictions to food, bevvies and drugs. Get your mind straight and follow your creative path!

Exercise: Close your eyes and breathe deeply through your nose with your mouth closed. Exhale through your nose. Do this for four cycles...deep breathes, deep exhales. Visualize your ideal future. Imagine what life would look like to you if you could do anything or all the things that nourish your Spirit. Hold that. Feel it. Keep breathing. Open your eyes. Write it down. Look at what you wrote. This is the direction to move toward. This is your art. It's probably frightening. In fact, if it is truly that path that gives you goosebumps of glee, it is without a doubt, scaring you right now. Perfect! That's when you know it's right. If you aren't feeling fear, you are living in complacency...and certainly not living your making. Take your next steps. Make the move. You got this!

Acknowledgements

Special thanks to:

Alyssa Maneval ~ Editor
Sarah Karasek ~ Editor
Quincey Morton-Swartz ~ Cover design & layout, Photography, Interior layout & Typesetting

You all ROCK!

About the Author

Kirsten is a Holistic Health Coach, a plant-based chef and cafe owner, a writer, a lover of life, an organic farmer and a wanderlust junkie. She transcends the ordinary, is a native of the land of the misfit toys and is not likely to ever be satisfied with "normal." Currently, she lives with her husband and doggie in Pennsylvania in their super cool converted school bus.

Kirsten is always seeking to work with like-minded individuals, coach those that want to better their physical and spiritual well-being, and travel for speaking engagements and workshops.

To contact Kirsten, please visit:
www.fortheloveofthejourney.com
www.kirstentonja.com
or email **kirstentonja@gmail.com**

Notes

Notes

Notes

Notes

Notes

www.ingramcontent.com/pod-product-compliance
Lightning Source LLC
LaVergne TN
LVHW051353080426
835509LV00020BB/3422